DATE			

Adaptation

Steve Parker

Heinemann Library
Chicago, Illinois

Designed by Celia Floyd
Originated by Dot Gradations
Printed by Wing King Tong, in Hong Kong

05 04 03 02 01

10 9 8 7 6 5 4 3 2 1

Library of Congress Cataloging-in-Publication Data
Parker, Steve, 1961-
      Adaptation / Steve Parker.
            p. cm. -- (Life processes)
      Includes bibliographical references (p.).
      ISBN 1-57572-335-2 (lib.)
      1. Adaptation (Biology)--Juvenile literature. [1. Adaptation (Biology)] I. Title.

QH546 .G36 2000
578.4--dc21

00-040937

Acknowledgments
The author and publishers are grateful to the following for permission to reproduce copyright
material: Bruce Coleman Collection/Mary Plage, p. 14; Corbis/Daniel Samuel Robbins, p. 9; NHPA,
p. 20; NHPA/B & C Alexander, p. 22; NHPA/A.N.T., pp. 7, 24; NHPA/Anthony Bannister, p. 11, 25;
NHPA/N. A. Callow, p. 4; NHPA/G. J. Cambridge, p. 18; NHPA/Vincente Gardia Canseco, p. 29;
NHPA/Stephen Dalton, pp. 10, 16, 28; NHPA/Martin Harvey, pp. 12, 15; NHPA/Daniel Heuclin, p.
25; NHPA/David Hosking, p. 27; NHPA/E. A. Janes, p. 19; NHPA/Darek Karp, p. 8; NHPA/David
Middleton, p. 4; NHPA/Dr. Eckart Pott, p. 13; NHPA/John Shaw, p. 23; NHPA/Hellio & Van Ingen,
p. 17; NHPA/Roy Waller, p. 19; NHPA/Norbert Wu, p. 21; Oxford Scientific Films/ Daniel J. Cox, p.
4; Oxford Scientific Films/Michael Fogden, p. 10; Oxford Scientific Films/Richard Herrmann, p. 20;
Oxford Scientific Films/Roland Mayr, p. 26; Oxford Scientific Films/Colin Milkins, p. 6; Oxford
Scientific Films/Sean Morris, p. 27.

Cover photograph reproduced with permission of Tony Stone.

Every effort has been made to contact copyright holders of any material reproduced in this book.
Any omissions will be rectified in subsequent printings if notice is given to the publisher.

Some words are shown in bold, **like this.** You can find out what they mean by looking
in the glossary.

Contents

Introduction

The living world is incredibly diverse. Living things, called **organisms,** range from jelly-like **microbes** to worms and insects, flowers and fish, lizards and birds, massive whales and giant trees. But most organisms cannot live just anywhere. Each one has features that help it survive in its surroundings, or **habitat.** These features are known as **adaptations.**

A Variety of Habitats

The world has many different types of **habitats,** such as mountains, lakes, woods, and seashores. Most animals, plants, and other living things are **adapted** to one particular habitat. This is so common and natural that we rarely notice it. But if we picture a living thing in the wrong habitat, the idea of adaptation becomes more obvious.

Suppose that a dolphin and a camel suddenly swapped places. The dolphin would not last long in a baking desert, with no water and too much heat. A camel could not survive in the open sea. It can hardly swim and would soon drown. Neither type of animal is adapted to the other's habitat.

The dolphin's smooth, streamlined body slips swiftly through the sea.

Small creatures like shieldbugs are colored to blend into their surroundings so that they are noticed less by **predators.**

Needs for survival

Living things have certain needs or requirements from their habitat, if they are to survive. These include:

- Energy to power their life processes. Plants obtain their energy from sunlight, and animals get theirs from food.
- Raw materials and **nutrients** for growth, body maintenance, and repair. Animals get these from food; plants get them from air and soil.
- Oxygen, the invisible gas in the air around us. Almost all living things need oxygen to survive.
- Water—life cannot exist without it.
- Shelter and protection from bad conditions, such as harsh weather, and also from predators.

Coniferous tree branches can flex and slope down so that snow slips off without piling up and breaking the tree.

- A mate for breeding. This is not vital for an individual to stay alive, but it is essential if its kind, or **species,** is to continue.

In each habitat, living things face challenges in meeting these needs. This book shows how they have adapted to face such challenges and survive in many different habitats.

On the move

One example of an adaptation is a body feature that enables an animal to move effectively in its habitat. For example:

- A fish has a broad tail and fins to push itself through the water.
- A bird has flapping wings to carry it through the air.
- A mole has broad, strong front paws to dig through soil.
- A gazelle has long legs to run swiftly across the grasslands.
- A monkey has long, flexible limbs with grasping hands and feet to swing through the forest branches.

Changing Conditions

Conditions in a **habitat** are always changing. Each day the sun rises, bringing light and warmth. The weather brings changes such as winds, storms, frost, and snow. On the seashore the tides rise and fall. These are all changes in the non-living world. Changes also happen in the living world. Sometimes animals like locusts, lemmings, or rabbits breed in vast numbers. They eat so much that other animals, who normally eat the same food, begin to starve. If living things are to survive, they must cope with all these varying conditions.

The barnacle's life is ruled by the twice-daily rise and fall of the tides.

Hot and cold

Every day the temperature rises and falls as the sun rises and sets. Most animals are **cold-blooded,** and their activity is greatly affected by the surrounding temperature. After a cool night, a snake crawls slowly into the morning sun and basks in its rays. Soon the snake is warm enough to move quickly to pursue prey. As dusk falls and the temperature drops, the snake cools down again and can only move slowly. So it hides under a sheltering rock for the night.

Similar animals, different adaptations

There are many examples of similar creatures, from the same animal group, that are **adapted** to different habitats.

● The African hare and American jackrabbit have very long legs and ears, and short fur. These features help the hare's body to lose warmth in the very hot conditions of its desert home.

● The Arctic hare has shorter legs and ears, and very long, thick fur. These features help to prevent loss of body warmth in the very cold habitat of the far north.

Adapted to the dark

The daily changes in light levels also affect many living things. Some animals are **nocturnal,** that is, active at night. They include moths, mice, owls, and bats. These animals have different adaptions to find their way in the dark. For example, a bat's high-pitched squeals bounce off nearby objects, revealing its location and helping it find food.

Mice, which are nocturnal, have huge eyes and long whiskers that help them find their way in the dark.

Types of adaptations

- Overall shape—A worm is long and thin to help it burrow through soil. A leaf is broad and flat to catch the most sunlight.
- Color and pattern—The green tree frog can sit unnoticed among green leaves.
- Body parts—The long fangs of a viper stab **venom** into its prey.
- Internal processes—The presence of a natural chemical **anti-freeze** in the bodies of ice worms allows them to live in the freezing temperatures inside glaciers.

Similar adaptations, different animals

There are many examples of animals from different groups that have similar adaptations because they live in the same habitat.

- Frogs, lizards, and squirrels that live in trees have long, slim, grasping fingers to hold on to the branches.
- Frogs, lizards, and squirrels that live on the ground have shorter, stubbier fingers to walk and run on hard surfaces.

Life in the Mountains

Unlike their surrounding lowlands, mountains are generally cold, wet, and windy. Very tall mountains have snow and ice on their upper slopes. Also, the air becomes thinner with height, so there is less of the vital gas oxygen that living things need to breathe. So the higher a mountain, the more severe its conditions for life. Mountain animals and plants are **adapted** in many ways to withstand these tough conditions.

Lower plant zones

On many mountains, plants grow at certain levels, or zones. There are broad-leaved woodlands at the base. The foothills are cloaked with conifer trees that have thin, tough, needle-like leaves to survive long, cold winters. Increasing cold, snow, and wind mean that tall trees cannot survive above a certain height, called the tree line. So the next highest zone may be bushy scrub with hardy plants such as heathers. These have tough leaves and woody stems that are less damaged by the strong winds.

Did you know?
- Yaks have the longest fur of any mammal, growing up to 39 inches in length.
- Plants such as edelweiss have fine hairs on their leaves to keep out cold and keep in moisture.

The alpine pasque flower, like the edelweiss, is adapted to harsh mountain conditions.

Up and down

Many larger mountain animals, like chamois in Europe and yak in Asia, make yearly journeys called **migrations.** In spring, they head for the higher slopes, where alpine meadow plants grow quickly in the summer warmth. In autumn, they return to the lower slopes and the shelter of the forests. **Predators** such as wolves and snow leopards follow them on the journey.

Yaks are adapted to living high up in the Himalaya mountains.

Higher plant zones

Above the scrub zone are short grasses and herbs, which make up the alpine meadow. These plants are low-growing, with cushion or rosette shapes, which helps them avoid fierce winds. Many alpine plants have developed adaptations like hairy leaves to keep out the worst of the frost and to keep in moisture. In the alpine meadow, the soil is thin, and rain quickly races away down the steep slopes. Higher still among the icy rocks and crags, no types of plant can survive.

Mountain animals

Small creatures such as insects and spiders can survive in the high mountains by feeding on bits and pieces of dead plants and animals, which are blown up the slopes by strong winds. Birds such as condors soar over the peaks watching for dead or dying victims. Many mountain mammals, such as chinchillas and vicunas in South America and yak in Asia, have very long, thick fur that keeps in body warmth. Like the mountain goat, chamois, and Siberian ibex, these mammals have strong legs and feet to help them grip the slippery rocks and ice as they speed across the steep slopes.

In the Forest

Regions with moist, tropical climates have ideal conditions for plant life. There is year-round warmth and light, plenty of water, and minerals and **nutrients** in the soil. The thriving variety of plants, in turn, supports a vast range of animals. These conditions make tropical forests the Earth's richest wildlife **habitats.** In contrast, there are other kinds of forests in which conditions are less favorable. Living things here have very different **adaptations.**

The macaw's bright colors and loud squawking warn other birds that this patch of tropical forest is occupied.

Plentiful life

The tropical-rainforest habitat is perfect for life in all shapes, forms, and colors. Plants and animals do not have to battle for survival against harsh physical conditions. But with so many life-forms packed so close together there are plenty of **predators; parasites;** competitors for food, shelter, and living space; and rivals for breeding. So living things must battle with each other rather than with the physical conditions.

The ground in a tropical forest is dark, so **epiphytic** plants like these bromeliads grow high up in the branches nearer the light.

Coping with cold

In **temperate** regions, winter is quiet time. Broad-leaved trees lose their leaves. Small animals like insects die off and leave tough-cased eggs to survive the cold. Dormice, marmots, and similar creatures **hibernate** or go into a deep winter sleep. Squirrels rest in their nests, coming out occasionally to dig up nuts and other food that they buried in autumn. Some small birds **migrate,** flying long distances to warmer regions. All of these are adaptations that help the animals survive the cold of winter.

Frozen solid

In the far north and south, winters are even longer and colder. Conifer trees like pines, firs, and spruce are adapted to these severe climates. Conifer leaves are small and tough and so resist frost and icy winds. Their sloping branches allow snow to slide off before it becomes too heavy and breaks the tree.

Animals, too, have many ways of surviving these long winters. Many types of frogs, salamanders, and reptiles can withstand being frozen almost solid. Their bodies have high levels of **anti-freeze** substances so they can thaw back to life in the spring.

How to hide in the forest

Many animals show amazing adaptations for **camouflage** by resembling parts of trees and bushes. They blend into the forest surroundings and are less obvious to predators or prey.

- Stick insects look like twigs.
- Leaf insects resemble green forest leaves.
- Thornbugs and scalebugs are shaped like tree thorns.
- Moths or butterflies resting on tree trunks look like bark or old leaves.
- Spiders and mantises have bright colors to blend in with flowers.

When looper caterpillars stand still, they look like small twigs. A spider has not recognized this caterpillar.

Rolling Grasslands

Where the climate is too dry for trees but too moist for a desert, grasses grow. They cover the land as far as the eye can see. The grassland **habitat** supports a huge quantity of life. But there are few trees or bushes to provide shade and shelter, and many animals struggle to survive the long, dry season. There is also the ever-present risk of brushfire or sudden flooding when the rains come.

Large plains mammals, like pronghorn in North America and giraffes and eland in Africa, have long legs to race away from predators.

The prairies

On the grasslands or **prairies** of North America, the largest animals are bison. These grazers have wide, flat teeth for munching grass all day. Their huge size and practice of living in herds are **adaptations** against such **predators** as wolves. Like many large grazers, bison **migrate** from a dry region to find better grazing elsewhere. Unfortunately, the number of bison were hugely reduced by human hunters and the use of the prairies for farming. On African grasslands called savannahs, zebra and wildebeest have similar herd-dwelling lives.

Big birds

Grasslands and open scrub are home to the world's largest birds. These are ostriches in Africa, emus in Australia, and rheas on the grasslands of South America. None of these birds can fly. But they all have long, powerful legs to help them run swiftly and escape from predators, and sharp toe claws they use to kick out in defense.

Dung beetles collect and bury dung from grassland mammals as food for their developing grubs.

Living low down

Smaller grassland animals have fewer defenses against predators, so many dig tunnels and burrows. In North America, prairie dogs form huge underground townships. As several prairie dogs feed on the surface, a few are always watching for danger. They yip and bark if a predator comes near. African naked mole rats stay in their tunnel networks their whole lives. These strange mammals live in **colonies** like bees or ants. Only one female, called the queen, mates. The others, who dig tunnels and gather plant roots and other food, are called workers.

City in the countryside

Termites are small, pale, thin-skinned insects that would soon die in hot sun. So they adapt small patches of grassland for their own needs. They build a tall mound from mud that dries hard, and dig a huge nest underneath. Here a million or more termites live in a cool, moist, underground city. Snakes, foxes, and even cheetahs use the mounds for shelter, and owls and other birds perch on them.

Did you know?

Some animals and plants, such as acacia trees and ants, have special relationships. The ants bite and sting animals who try to eat the tree's leaves. In return, the thorny acacia provides the ants with a protected place to live. This type of relationship, where both partners benefit, is called **symbiosis**.

Flowing Waters

A typical river is not one **habitat** but many. Different animals and plants are **adapted** to these different parts of the river. In the hills, its gathering waters rush fast and foamy over a stony bed. When the river reaches lower plains, it **meanders,** or flows in wide loops, and its current decreases so that sand and silt collect along the banks. As the river enters the sea at its **estuary,** it slows still further, and its fresh water mixes with salty seawater.

The young river

Near the river's beginning the fast current sweeps away small plants, animals, and bits of food. However, a few animals are suited to these conditions. Stonefly **larvae** have low, flattened bodies and strong, wide-set, clawed legs that help them grip the pebbles on the bottom. Fish called bullheads also have low, flat bodies and also hide among the stones, where the river flow is slower.

Dippers are land birds that have adapted to diving for food in fast-flowing upland streams.

The mature river

As the river's waters slow, **nutrient**-rich mud collects on the bottom and bank. Plants such as reeds and rushes take root, providing food and shelter. Larger predatory fish like perch and pike thrive here, eating the plentiful smaller prey of worms, water insects, and young fish. Catfish and crayfish come out from their holes at night to **scavenge.**

The estuary

Near the sea, the fresh river water mixes with the sea's salty water. Salty water can cause great problems for freshwater animals since it greatly affects their body chemistry. Certain fish, such as mullet, are adapted to this in-between watery world. So are shellfish like winkles, oysters, and mussels.

Altering the habitat

Beavers, like other rodents such as rats and squirrels, have large front teeth for gnawing. They gnaw down branches and small trees and drag these into a stream to form a wall-like dam. The water builds up behind into a pool. Here the beavers build a house or lodge from twigs, mud, and stones, safe from **predators** like wolves, coyotes, and lynx.

Mangrove swamps

Along some sheltered tropical coasts, mangroves form huge swamps. The thick seashore mud contains little oxygen. But mangrove trees have roots that stick up into the air and water to take in extra oxygen. Mudskippers are also adapted to this habitat. These small fish hold pools of water in their large **gill** chambers, so they can survive in air for many minutes. Their front fins are like muscular arms and they use them to skitter across the mudflats.

Many large fish swim into coastal mangrove swamps to lay their eggs in the sheltered waters.

Did you know?

The world's largest reptile lives in estuaries and mangrove swamps, mainly around the Indian and west Pacific Oceans. What is it? The saltwater or estuarine crocodile, which grows to be more than 26 feet long.

Lakes and Ponds

Unlike a fast river, a lake or pool has still water. So it does not have the problems of a fast current and a lack of places to shelter. But cold, moving water takes in more oxygen from the air than warm, still water. Tropical lakes and marshes may look ideal for wildlife, but animals and plants find survival difficult in their **stagnant,** oxygen-poor water.

Rat-tailed maggots, **larvae** of hoverflies, survive in stagnant water by breathing air through a long tail tube.

Breathing

Creatures deal with the lack of oxygen with various **adaptations.** In the Amazon's tropical swamps, some fish can gulp air into their **swim bladders.** The blood-rich linings of these body parts absorb oxygen from the swallowed air, like the lungs of a land animal do. One of the world's biggest freshwater fish, the arapaima, which grows more than 6 feet long, uses this method. Lungfish have body parts that are even more adapted for breathing air. They live in South America, Africa, and Australia. They are long, slim fish resembling eels. Lung fish grow to about 5 feet long and hunt smaller fish, frogs, and other water creatures. They absorb oxygen from air when their pools become shallow and stagnant.

Blood red

On a much smaller scale, worms called blood- or sludgeworms also survive in low-oxygen water, even polluted ponds. They live half-buried in tubes on the bottom, their bright tail ends waving in the water. These animals get their color from extra amounts of the oxygen-carrying substance **hemoglobin** in their blood, the same substance that makes our blood red.

Adapted for lurking

Air-breathing animals of lakes and swamps do not face the problem of low oxygen levels in water. But they still need to obtain food. The top **predators** in this habitat are crocodiles and alligators. Their body shape is adapted to lurking almost submerged in water. The nostrils and eyes on the top of the head allow the crocodile to breathe, smell, and watch for prey. Their long jaws and many teeth grab victims in a vice-like grip. These supreme hunters have been around for more than 200 million years, since the time of the dinosaurs.

The flamingo's special beak has comb-like flaps inside to strain food from water and mud.

17

Tides and Waves

Coasts and seashores have the world's most varying conditions. Twice each day, the sea level rises at high tide and floods the area with salty water. Waves crash forcefully onto the shore. As the tide falls, living things are exposed to hot sun, drying winds, freshwater rain, or icy frosts. Added to all this are the usual changes of day and night and the yearly cycle of seasons. Animals and plants that live in this kind of habitat have extremely specialized **adaptations,** and most cannot live anywhere else.

Shorefish like blennies and minnows have tough, rubbery, slippery skin that prevents damage by waves and rolling pebbles.

Tough plants

Plants along the coast consist mainly of **algae** called *seaweeds*. They do not have roots like land plants, but many have root-like **holdfasts** that cling to the rocks so they are not swept away by waves. Seaweeds also have leaf-like **fronds** with tough, slippery surfaces that are not torn by the waves or dried out by the sun.

Ruled by the tide

Most seashore animals are not adapted to the 24-hour cycle of day and night. Instead, they follow the 12-hour cycle of the tides. Crabs, shrimps, prawns, sea snails, and worms are all active at high tide and hide away for low tide.

Some animals stay under the mud or sand. They include shellfish like scallops, cockles, and clams. As the tide comes in they extend fleshy tubes called **siphons.** Shellfish suck in water through one siphon, filter out tiny edible particles inside their bodies, and squirt the water out of the other siphon.

Sea anemones extend their tentacles to catch prey, then as the tide falls they close up like flowers.

Holding onto the rocks

Animals of the seashore are also at risk of being swept away. Crabs, fish, and other animals find shelter in crevices or among seaweeds. Sea snails have a broad foot for sticking to the rocks. The limpet has the strongest grip and does not need to find shelter. It can clamp its low, cone-shaped shell to the rock with a force that resists the strongest waves.

At low tide, seaweeds provide cool, moist shelter for seashore animals like this crab.

Trapped for life

On the shore the tides, waves, and currents continually bring seawater containing two of life's essentials—food and oxygen. Piddocks are shellfish that burrow into solid rock by twisting and rasping their strong, spiny shells. As in other shellfish, two siphons take in water for feeding and breathing and then squirt it out. The piddock grows as it bores slowly into the rock so that it becomes too big to leave its tunnel.

Did you know?

The lugworm, in its u-shaped burrow, eats sand to digest any **nutrient** particles. It ejects the grains onto the surface above its rear end as squiggly worm casts. In one year, a lugworm can eat enough sand to fill a family car!

Life in the Ocean

The ocean is the largest **habitat** on Earth. It is bigger than all other habitats combined. Where its warm, shallow waters lap calmly toward a tropical beach, this may seem ideal for life. But the ocean also has huge waves and strong currents. About 1,600–3,200 feet below the surface, the ocean is cold and dark. Plants, so vital to animal survival, cannot grow. This presents many challenges to living things.

Sea lions in the warm, tropical waters off the coast of California.

Small plants, big fish

The main plants in the ocean are microscopic **phytoplankton.** They provide food for similarly small animals, **zooplankton.** Larger animals have **adaptations** to feed on such tiny food. The two biggest fish in the world, the whale shark and the basking shark, filter them from the water using frilly, comb-like parts called **rakers.** These are on the **gills,** the breathing parts on the side of a fish's head.

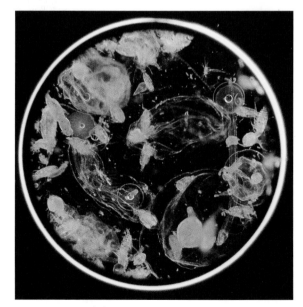

Zooplankton provide a source of food for the whale shark.

Life at the surface

These huge fish have enormous livers made of oily flesh. Oil is lighter than water, and the large liver helps the fish stay near the surface where plankton is richest. However, the sperm whale has the opposite problem. It is a mammal and so must surface to breathe air. But its prey of large fish and giant squid live far below the surface. So the sperm whale has great quantities of a waxy substance, **spermacetti,** in its bulging forehead. As the whale dives, the spermacetti becomes more solid and heavier, helping the whale to descend more than 900 feet.

Did you know?
The female deep-sea anglerfish has no trouble finding a male mate in the vast, black ocean depths. He attaches onto her body and stays there, living on her like a **parasite,** and always ready for breeding.

On the deep ocean bed

More than seven-eighths of the ocean is cold and pitch dark. The only food there is dead bodies, droppings, and other things that have drifted down from above. Most of the creatures on the bottom, such as sea-cucumbers, worms, clams, and other shellfish, are blind. They have no eyes since there is no light to see. Instead, their bodies are sensitive to touch and water currents. They feed on small edible pieces in the thick seabed mud.

Grab any prey you can

Animals are rare in the vast, black depths of the sea. So deep-sea fish that hunt there are adapted to grab almost any prey they find. The gulper eel has a mouth that is five times bigger than its body. The viperfish has long, sharp teeth that angle backward into its throat so that any prey it grabs cannot escape.

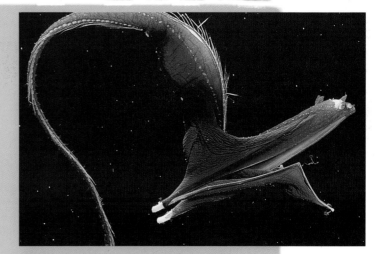

The deep-sea gulper eel has a gigantic mouth.

Survival Near the Poles

Some of the harshest conditions for life on Earth are found in polar lands. In the far north, the ice-covered Arctic Ocean is surrounded by frozen lands. In the south, chilly seas surround the icy continent of Antarctica. The main problems there are intense cold and long, dark winters. Few plants can grow in such conditions, and this means there is little food for animals. The cold, treeless plains of grasses, sedges, and other low plants are known as the **tundra habitat.**

Reindeer walk long distances **migrating,** north for summer plant growth, then south for winter shelter.

Short summers, long winters

The polar regions have the most extreme climates in the world. For a short time each summer the sun never sets, and the temperature rises to several degrees above freezing. Conditions are suitable for life. But during the long winter, the sun hardly rises, and the air temperature can fall below minus 120° Fahrenheit. Within seconds, any living thing can freeze solid.

Summer visitors

The winter in polar lands is too long, cold, and dark for most larger animals. So they migrate to warmer places. In the Arctic, many kinds of ducks, geese, plovers, and similar birds fly south to warmer regions for the winter. They return north again the next spring to nest and raise their young.

Coping with winter

Plants and animals in polar regions have made **adaptations** to cope with the intense winter cold and to take advantage of the brief summer growing season. The main plants are sedges and mosses. They are low-growing and so are protected from the fierce wind. Small animals like springtails, midges, mosquitoes, and other insects survive the winter as tough-cased eggs that hatch in spring.

Warm white coats

Warm-blooded Arctic animals include such birds as snowy owls and ptarmigan, and such mammals as polar bears, seals, voles, snowshoe hares, and Arctic foxes. They have extra-thick coats of feathers or fur and a thick layer of fat under the skin, called **blubber,** to keep in body warmth. Most spend the long winter resting in sheltered nests in burrows, caves, or dens.

Ptarmigan change their white winter plumage to brown for **camouflage** in summer.

In polar seas

The seas around Antarctica are very cold. However, they are also extremely rich in **nutrients** brought up from deeper waters by ocean currents. In summer, the seas support a wide variety of life that starts with the tiny plants and animals of the plankton. These are eaten by small fish and shrimp-like creatures known as **krill.** In turn, these animals are eaten by squid, larger fish, penguins, seals, and whales.

Did you know?
The largest animals that live permanently on the mainland of Antarctica are tiny springtails, insects that are just a tiny fraction of an inch long.

Heat and Drought

Deserts may be hot or cold, sandy or rocky, windy or calm, in highlands or lowlands. But all deserts have one feature in common—lack of water, or **drought.** Since water is vital for any form of life, deserts pose huge problems for animals and plants. Yet even in these dry wastes, living things have developed amazing **adaptations** and found ways to survive.

The desert comes alive

For years, the desert may look brown and lifeless. Then within a few days of rain, plants begin to spring up. They have been **dormant** or inactive, either as seeds or as underground bulbs or **corms.** Such plants, called **ephemerals,** are adapted to grow quickly and produce flowers and seeds while the soil is moist.

There are also ephemeral animals. Fairy shrimps survive drought as tough-cased eggs. These hatch quickly, grow into adults in temporary puddles, and breed to produce the next batch of eggs. Their whole life cycle is over within a few days as the desert dries out once more.

The water-holding frog of Australia survives drought underground in a watery, bag-like cocoon.

Gathering moisture

The main challenge in the desert is to find water. Plants like cacti spread their long, thin roots far and wide to soak up moisture from a large surface area. Cacti's leaves are sharp spines—an adaptation that protects against plant-eating animals and moisture loss. Their stems are wide and barrel-shaped to store water. Trees such as acacias and baobabs send roots many feet down into the soil to find moisture far below.

The darkling beetle stands on its head to catch morning dew and mist on its body. The liquid runs down into its mouth.

Out at night

Many desert creatures avoid the scorching daytime sun by coming out only during twilight or at night. By day, smaller animals like desert mice and kangaroo rats hide in cool burrows. Larger animals, such as kangaroos and Arabian oryx, rest in the shade of a tree, rock, or dune. These creatures obtain most of the moisture they need from leaves and seeds.

Moving over soft sand

Soft desert sand tends to shift and slip as animals move over it, so various desert creatures have adapted their bodies to different ways of moving.

- Kangaroo rats, gerbils, and jerboas have large back feet and leap rather than run.
- Camels have wide feet that spread their body weight and keep them from sinking.
- Desert sidewinder snakes move in a sideways fashion almost like waves rippling on the beach. Their long bodies push against the sand, giving a larger surface area so the sand grains slip less.

- Such lizards as desert skinks and sandfish do not walk on the surface at all. They wriggle through the sand, almost like fish swimming through water.

Dromedary camels in the Sahara Desert.

Living on the Edge

A few places in the world seem too harsh and inhospitable to support any form of life. They include the ice and snow of glaciers and icebergs, hot springs with their near-boiling water, and deep dark caves. Yet even in these places, living things have **adapted** and found ways to survive—and in some cases, to thrive. **Organisms** that adapt to these severe conditions have few **predators,** competitors, or rivals. This is why extreme **habitats** have only a few **species** of animals or plants, but those species have great numbers.

Life after death

After a brush fire, **pioneer** plants grow rapidly in the blackened earth. They are not adapted for a long stay. Gradually they are crowded out by slower, steadier growers. However, by then they have already grown, flowered, and scattered their seeds widely.

Large trees such as black spruce, wild ginger, and labrador have adaptations such as thick bark that resists fire damage. Underground parts of herbs like sage, thyme, and rosemary also survive scorching.

Pioneer plants have sprung up here following a brush fire in Yellowstone National Park, Wyoming.

Did you know?

A new island called Surtsey appeared in the North Atlantic near Iceland in 1963. At first it was bare, hot rock. However, by the year 2000, more than 1,000 species of plants and animals lived there.

Invading new land

Brand new land, like an ocean island made by a just-erupted underwater volcano, rarely stays empty. Plant seeds blow in the wind, like those of the *Brachycereus* cactus that grows on new volcanic rocks. Sea creatures such as seals and turtles climb out and leave their **nutrient**-rich droppings. Visiting birds bring tiny eggs and small animals on their bodies and plant seeds and more nutrients in their droppings. Tiny creatures like mites and spiders also blow in on the wind. Gradually, the bare land develops into a thriving habitat.

When warmth kills

Grylloblattids are strange insects found in remote mountains such as the North American Rockies. They look like a combination of cockroach and cricket, but they are a separate insect group. Grylloblattids live on glaciers and snowfields, scavenging on windblown scraps of food. Their body processes are adapted to thrive at temperatures of about 32–41° Fahrenheit. If they become much warmer, they die.

A grylloblattid

Extremes of heat and cold

The water of some hot springs is too scalding to touch. Yet **extremophile** organisms like **bacteria** and **algae** grow and form crusts on the rocks. At the other end of the temperature scale are ice-worms, which burrow through the ice of Alaska, and bacteria that live on the undersides of icebergs. These simple organisms contain unusual versions of substances called **enzymes,** which break down minerals in the surroundings to get the energy for life.

Colorful hot springs support heat-loving organisms.

The Urban Jungle

The fastest-spreading **habitats** in the world are towns and cities. Bricks, concrete, asphalt, and mown grass may seem hostile and forbidding to wild animals and plants. Indeed, most cannot survive here. But the urban habitat has some features that are similar to certain natural surroundings. This is why certain plants and animals have **adapted** to town and city life. Others have done so well that people have come to regard them as pests.

City cliffs and crags

In the wild, rock doves live and nest around cliffs and crags. The urban habitat has similar places—the walls and ledges of buildings. This similarity led rock doves to move into towns, where they feasted on leftovers and waste food. Gradually, the doves became urban inhabitants. Today, hundreds of major cities have large populations of their descendants, known as **feral** pigeons.

At home in the town

A similar story has been repeated for various other animals and plants that are now familiar urban dwellers. Creatures include house mice, brown rats, gray squirrels, red foxes, gulls, starlings, house sparrows, blackbirds, spiders, ants, termites, cockroaches, and the commonest of all, house flies. In many tropical regions, animals such as geckos and tree frogs also find their way into houses. Plants include dandelions, thistles, and shrubs like elder and buddleia.

Birds like this robin will happily nest in quiet buildings or sheds.

Taking the opportunity

The wildlife that moves into towns and cities is described as **opportunistic.** It takes advantage of the surroundings we create for ourselves. All the essentials of life are found in developed areas, such as warmth in our centrally-heated buildings and shelter in our roof spaces, hollow walls, pipes, and drains. And of course their is plentiful food, either stored for our use or thrown away in dumpsters. The animals have adapted, too. They change their behavior and diet, taking the opportunity to eat what is available and nesting wherever they can.

Up on the roof

Barns, churches, and other big buildings are like great tree holes or caves for animals. They have become homes for different animals around the world:

- Racoons in North America.
- Roof rats in parts of Asia.
- Ring-tailed possums in Australia.
- Barn owls almost everywhere, making them the world's most common bird.

Did you know?

One of the world's biggest feathered pests is the red-billed quelea. Millions of these birds devastate farm crops all across the continent of Africa.

Many animals, especially such natural **scavengers** as gulls and rats, fit in well in urban habitats. The garbage dump is like a vast supermarket for them, full of a variety of foods.

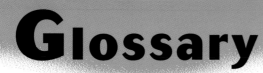Glossary

adaptation   change in a feature of a living thing that helps it to fit into its surroundings, or environment, and improve its chances of survival

algae   one-celled plant found in both saltwater and freshwater

antifreeze   chemical substance that does not freeze solid when it becomes very cold

bacteria   living thing, only visible under a microscope, and found almost everywhere on Earth

blubber   oily or fatty layer under the skin of certain animals that helps to keep in body warmth

camouflage   blending in with the surroundings, usually by shape, color, or pattern, to be less noticeable

cold-blooded   animals, including fish, amphibians, and reptiles, that cannot control their own body temperature and rely on the weather to warm them up or cool them down

colony   members of a species of animal that live fairly close together in one area

corm   underground part of a plant, similar to a bulb, that stores plant nutrients during the winter

dormant   still, inactive, and not changing much

drought   long time without rain or some other form of moisture

enzyme   natural chemical substance inside living things that causes bodily changes

ephemeral   short-lived, fleeting, soon gone

epiphytic   type of plant that grows on another one and uses it to gain height, support, and perhaps shelter

estuary   river's mouth, where it opens out wide and flows into the ocean

extremophile   living thing that thrives in harsh conditions, such as great heat or intense cold

feral   animal that was once tame or domesticated but has escaped to become partly wild again

gill   1) thin body part that fish use for breathing 2) fine ridge on the underside of a mushroom or toadstool's cap where spores grow

grazer   animal that eats or grazes on grass

habitat   distinctive type of place or surroundings, such as a woodland, mountain top, grassland, pond, or seashore

hemoglobin   red substance in the blood that absorbs and carries oxygen around the body

hibernate   to becomes inactive and go into a sleeplike state during winter

holdfast   part by which a plant clings to a flat surface

krill   small sea creatures in the same family as shrimps

larva   young form of insect that looks very different from the adults—plural is larvae

meander   wide curve or bend in a river

microbe   tiny microorganism, like bacteria, that can only be seen under a microscope

migrate, migration   to make a long journey as seasons change to find more food or better shelter

nocturnal   animal that is active at night, like bats, cats, and owls

nutrient   substance needed by a living thing for its growth, development, and survival

opportunistic   taking advantage of any chance that comes along

organism   scientific word for a living thing

parasite   plant or animal that lives on or in another plant or animal and gets all its food from it

phytoplankton   microscopic, single-celled plants that live in the sea and form the start of the ocean food chain

pioneer   first or earliest individual in a new place

prairie   large region of grassland where there are few trees

predator   animal that hunts and kills other animals for food

raker   comb-like part on the gills of a water animal that filters tiny bits of food from the water

scavenger   animal that feeds on the dead bodies of other animals or plants

siphon   in an animal, a body opening shaped like a tube that takes water in or passes it out, usually during breathing or feeding

species   group of living things that look similar to each other and can breed together, but that cannot breed with other living things

spermaceti   waxy or oily substance inside the head of the sperm whale that helps it to dive to great depths

stagnant   still, old, or stale, rather than fresh and new

symbiosis   relationship between two different living things that benefits both of them

swim bladder   part of a water creature, such as a fish, that contains air and helps the animal swim, rise, and descend in the water

temperate   having cold winters and warm summers

tundra   flat, treeless region in a very cold place, where the soil is frozen solid for part of the year

urban   relating to towns, cities, or developed areas

venom   poison

warm-blooded   animals that can control their own body temperature so that it stays the same no matter how hot or cold it is

zooplankton   tiny sea animals that graze on phytoplankton

More Books to Read

Capon, Brian. *Plant Survival: Adapting to a Hostile World.* Portland, Oreg.: Timber Press, 1994.

Kalman, Bobbie and Jaqueline Langville. *How Do Animals Adapt?* New York: Crabtree Publishing Co., 2000.

Markham-David, Sally. *It Takes All Kinds.* DeSoto, Tex.: McGraw-Hill, 1994.

Index